gospel-centred

Family

*becoming the parents
God wants you to be*

Ed Moll Tim Chester

thegoodbook
COMPANY

Gospel-centred family
© 2009 Tim Chester and Ed Moll/The Good Book Company.
Reprinted 2010, 2011
All rights reserved.

The Good Book Company
Tel: 0333 123 0880; **International:** +44 (0) 208 942 0880
Email: admin@thegoodbook.co.uk

Websites:
UK: www.thegoodbook.co.uk
N America: www.thegoodbook.com
Australia: www.thegoodbook.com.au
New Zealand: www.thegoodbook.co.nz

ISBN: 9781906334703

Cover design: Steve Devane
Printed in China

Contents

Introduction

Children are great. No, really, they are. Of course, they sometimes drive us up the wall. (Just mine then?) But we still love them to bits.

Parents are great too. It's true that a few are abusive. But most have a profound love for their children. Of course, we're fallible. Make that *very* fallible (even if we do claim mummy knows best). But we try to do our best for our children.

Parenting is tough. Families offer security, acceptance, safety, love. But they can also be places of conflict, defiance, suspicion.

This is a book about gospel-centred families. The word "gospel" means "good news". So this is a book offering good news for families. It offers ideas to help you negotiate the sometimes troubled waters of family life.

But our good news is more than good advice. It's more than tips based on experience. It's about the good news of life, hope, forgiveness and freedom in Jesus, and how this good news impacts family life.

The Bible isn't a manual on parenting. You can't look under "D" for "discipline" or "T" for "teenagers". The Bible is a story – the story of God's salvation. It tells the story of the creation of the world, the rebellion of humanity, the promises God made to Israel and the coming of God's Son, Jesus. It tells us how God designed the world, what's gone wrong and how God is putting the world right again through Jesus.

This book shows how this wonderful story intersects with the story of your family. The Bible story can become the story of what God designed your family to be, what goes wrong in your family and how God can put your family right again through His Son, Jesus.

There are two common, contrasting approaches to parenting. Some people emphasise that every family is different and so parents need to make it up as they go along. Other people emphasise biblical absolutes and so prescribe precise techniques. The reality is there are biblical absolutes, but at the level of principles rather than processes. Good parenting is not about adopting certain techniques. It's about living as part of God's story and letting God's good news shape your values, attitudes and behaviour.

Families come in all different shapes and sizes. Two parents, single parents, step-parents. Several children, an only child, step-children. We tried not to assume every family fits the two parents with 2.4 children mould. We recognise that single parents face extra challenges while step-children raise their own unique issues. But to make life easier we'll sometimes speak of your child, sometimes of your children; of a parent and parents.

One more thing before we begin. We've divided the book into lots of short chapters to make it easy to read between changing nappies and cleaning up sick or giving lifts and washing sports kit. The short chapters also mean you could read it as a couple after a long day.

If you want to read it as a group, you might consider combining chapters, though you may find you have enough to talk about together taking one chapter at a time. Don't have more than ten people for each leader. Parents can feel quite vulnerable talking about family life so agree to some ground rules: we will keep confidences, celebrate our children rather than talk them down, support our spouse rather than undermine them, submit to God's word rather than assume we're experts. Start with an activity that warms people up. Conclude with some time for people to identify specific changes they want to implement. And, because parenting often comes with a dose of guilt, end with a reminder of God's grace.

Finding your way around

 ## Consider this

A scenario—often based on a real-life situation—which raises some kind of dilemma or frustration in gospel ministry.

 ## Biblical background

A relevant Bible passage together with some questions to help you think it through.

 ## Read all about it

A discussion of the principle, both in terms of its theological underpinning and its contemporary application.

 ## Questions for reflection

Questions that can be used for group discussion or personal reflection.

 ## Ideas for action

Some ideas or an exercise to help people think through the application of the principle to their own situation.

We have tried to make this book work:

- whether it is read by an individual or used as the basis for group discussion.

- whether you want to work through it systematically or turn to particular topics as they arise.

a gospel-centred family

1 Gospel-centred families

Your family can show how great it is to live under God's reign of love.

Consider this

Karen slumped onto the sofa.

"It's just the terrible twos," her friend had told her this morning. But there was no "just" about it. This was war! She loved Jack so much, but he was driving her mad. Refusing to eat. Throwing food on the floor. Pulling books off the shelves. Hitting his baby sister. Screaming on the supermarket floor. She'd tried reasoning with him. She'd tried negotiation. She'd tried bribery. Truth was she wasn't even sure what she was trying to achieve. It just felt like crisis management.

Then the baby monitor crackled into life. Here we go again.

"Is there more to parenting than survival?" she asked herself.

Biblical background

Read Ephesians 6 v 1-4

- ❓ What is expected from children and parents?
- ❓ Why should children obey their parents?
- ❓ What does it mean for parents to "exasperate" their children? Can you think of examples?
- ❓ Why does the writer point out that this commandment is the first with a promise?
- ❓ What does this passage suggest is the purpose of families?

Read all about it

Show that God's rule is good

"Jesus went into Galilee, proclaiming the good news of God. 'The time has come,' he said. 'The kingdom of God is near. Repent and believe the good news!'" (Mark 1 v 14-15).

Jesus began His ministry by proclaiming the good news – or "gospel" – that the kingdom of God was near. God's kingdom was coming because God's King was coming. Good news. Gospel.

Except that the rule of God doesn't sound much like good news in our culture. No kind of rule sounds like good news. We want to be free. We don't want someone else ruling over us. How can the rule of God be good news? Surely God's rule is bad news.

This was the lie of Satan way back in the Garden of Eden when the "serpent" portrayed God as a tyrant holding Adam and Eve back. But God isn't a tyrant. His rule is a rule of blessing, freedom, love, life, justice and peace. Good news. Gospel.

But isn't this a book on parenting? What's this got to do with parenting? Everything.

Look at Ephesians 6 v 1-4. What's obeying parents got to do with living long in the land? Verses 2-3 are a quote from Deuteronomy 5 v 16, where Moses is recounting the Ten Commandments. He ends by saying: "So be careful to do what the Lord your God has commanded you; do not turn aside to the right or to the left. Walk in all the way that the Lord your God has commanded you, so that you may live and prosper and prolong your days in the land that you will possess" (Deuteronomy 5 v 32-33). God's people would live a life of blessing in God's land if they obeyed God. Anything else would lead to chaos, conflict and destruction. Ultimately, if they rejected God, they would not live long in the land – they'd be exiled (as it turned out they were). Welcoming God's rule = blessing. Rejecting God's rule = judgment.

That's true in families. When people in families live for themselves, the result is chaos, conflict and destruction. In families we learn to live alongside others, negotiate differences and express our views while tolerating other opinions. The Puritan Thomas Manton said: "The family is the seminary of church and state ... A failure in the first area will not be mended in the second."

But it's not just about having a happy family or a happy community.

The family is the place where you learn to submit to authority instead of living for yourself. In this section of Ephesians, Paul says our different roles in life are all to reflect God's role in our lives. Marriage is an illustration of Christ's relationship with His people (5 v 22-33), while working relationships are to be shaped by the fact that we are slaves of a Master in heaven (6 v 5-9). It's the same with families. Parents are God's gift to children to teach us how to live under authority. We learn to submit to authority instead of living for ourselves by learning to submit to our parents.

That's why this is the first commandment with a promise. Learning to enjoy your parents' authority is the first step towards welcoming God's authority.

Don't tell children off for being children. Children break things and drop things. They get giddy and raise their voices. But ensure they obey you. Teach them to submit to your authority. Discipline disobedience. Don't let your child rule the home. If you do, you'll be teaching them that they are king in their lives. They're not. It won't prepare them for wider social interaction. And it won't prepare them to meet the true King.

Let your child realise they're not the centre of the world. It's very easy, especially in early years, for children to be all-consuming. So invest in your relationship as a husband and wife. Not only does healthy parenting require a healthy marriage, it will also reinforce for your child that they're not the centre of the world, not even of your world!

Parents are to model God's good, liberating, just rule in the way they bring up their children. We're to show that it is good to live under authority. We're to show that authority can be good.

Show that God's rule is gracious

But hang on a moment. Is God's kingdom really good news? Not if you're a rebel! "Where is the God of justice?" people asked the prophet Malachi. He's on his way, said Malachi. "But who can endure the day of his coming?" (Malachi 2 v 17 – 3 v 2). For God's people His rule is good news, but for His enemies His rule means judgment and defeat. And we are all God's enemies. We've all opted to live our life our way without God.

The good news is that the coming of Jesus as God's King defied most people's expectations. It wasn't all about glory and conquest. That's coming when Jesus returns at the end of history. But when Jesus came first time round, judgment didn't fall. Or rather, it fell on the King Himself! The King died on the cross in the place of His enemies. God's rule is not only good, it's also gracious. God makes it possible for His enemies to become His friends.

Jesus told the story of a family in which the younger son rejected the authority of his father (Luke 15). He went off and squandered his part of the family's inheritance. But rejecting his father's authority didn't make him free or happy. He ended up wishing he could eat the food he was serving to pigs. So he decided to return to his father and ask if he could become a servant. But his father ran in a most undignified way to greet his returning son. He honoured his son with a robe and ring. He threw an extravagant party to welcome him home. God is a gracious Father who welcomes wayward children.

Often parenting can feel like a battle. And the "enemy" is your two-year-old who's just thrown their dinner on the floor (again); or your fifteen-year-old, who's just slammed the door on you (again). But still your job is to show them what our Father in heaven is like. Yes, they need to learn to live under authority. But they also need to learn of a God who welcomes His enemies, loves His enemies and gives His life for His enemies.

Your number one aim as a parent is to *show how great it is to live under God's reign of love*.

Questions for reflection

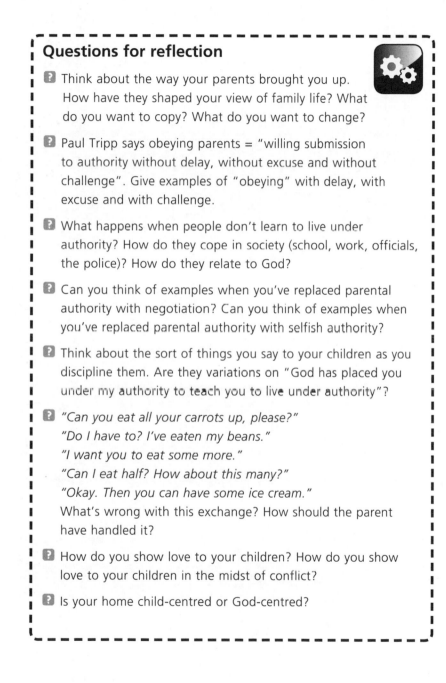

- ❓ Think about the way your parents brought you up. How have they shaped your view of family life? What do you want to copy? What do you want to change?

- ❓ Paul Tripp says obeying parents = "willing submission to authority without delay, without excuse and without challenge". Give examples of "obeying" with delay, with excuse and with challenge.

- ❓ What happens when people don't learn to live under authority? How do they cope in society (school, work, officials, the police)? How do they relate to God?

- ❓ Can you think of examples when you've replaced parental authority with negotiation? Can you think of examples when you've replaced parental authority with selfish authority?

- ❓ Think about the sort of things you say to your children as you discipline them. Are they variations on "God has placed you under my authority to teach you to live under authority"?

- ❓ *"Can you eat all your carrots up, please?"*
  "Do I have to? I've eaten my beans."
  "I want you to eat some more."
  "Can I eat half? How about this many?"
  "Okay. Then you can have some ice cream."
  What's wrong with this exchange? How should the parent have handled it?

- ❓ How do you show love to your children? How do you show love to your children in the midst of conflict?

- ❓ Is your home child-centred or God-centred?

2 Gospel-centred hopes

Knowing God is far more important than "succeeding" in life.

Consider this

Jamal has swimming lessons. Dave goes to scouts. Angela's learning the flute. Pete has a new games console. Kathy's part of a dance group. Leo's going to a special French tutor. Paul does archery. Sue has a pony.

Denise shops at *Gap for Kids*. Paula only gives her children organic food. Brian runs the football club. Carl bakes his own bread. Trevor's a school governor.

John has piano lessons, plays cricket, does extra homework, goes to drama group, is part of a model-aircraft club and sings in a choir. Something for every day of the week.

Hannah sees John's mum driving him to and from events all the time. It makes her feel anxious. Is she letting her Sam down? Maybe she should push him to do more. Some music lessons? A sports team? Extra homework? Some kind of club? A hobby? But what? What matters most?

Biblical background

Read Deuteronomy 6 v 4-9

- ❓ What is the link between verse 4 and verse 5?
- ❓ What are the people of Israel to teach their children?
- ❓ When are they to teach their children?
- ❓ What's the link between our lives and our teaching?
- ❓ What priorities does this passage suggest for parenting and family life?

Read all about it

What do you want for your children? A good education? Plenty of extra activities: scouts, football, dancing, music lessons, art club? The latest games console? What are your hopes for your children? A good career? A comfortable lifestyle? Safety and good health? Their own home? A happy marriage? Grandchildren?

Often our true values are revealed in the expectations we have for our children. On Sunday in church we sing about how knowing Jesus is the greatest thing. But our priorities and hopes for our children suggest that what matters most in life is educational development, career development, social development, skills development.

We often worry (rightly) about the influence the world has on our children. We worry about sex and drugs and rock "n" roll. But *we* are also influencing our children. And our influence can be just as corrosive of gospel-centred priorities. Knowing God is important to us, yes. After all, that's what we give our Sundays to. But what matters Monday to Friday is getting an education, making money, the career ladder, "succeeding" in life. And what matters on Saturday is pleasure and leisure. When we talk about our children, we don't talk about their love for Jesus or their Christian service. We talk about their schooling, their clubs or their prospects.

My wife's an infant school teacher. She has parents asking for extra homework. My friend coaches a boys' football team. The worst thing about it, he says, are the parents pushing their children to win at all costs. The bloke a few doors down from me gets his son to wash the car three times a week. It's clear what matters most to these parents. And that's what your children are learning is important in life.

Imagine your child aged 25. What do you imagine them doing? Succeeding in their career, buying a house, getting married and dutifully attending church each Sunday morning? Or do you imagine them as a gospel worker – planting a church, serving the community, glorifying God in the workplace, going overseas, telling people about Jesus and doing whatever job best enables them to do these things. Which comes first? Career or service? The way you answer that question will tell you a lot about what matters most in your life.

I've often heard people say they would consider living in the city, but they're concerned about their children's influences and education. But that begs the question: what do you want for your children? If you want them to be middle-class, prosperous and respectable, then live in a leafy suburb, send them to a good school and keep them away from messed-up people. But if you want them to serve Christ in a radical, whole-hearted way, then model that for them in the way you live. That won't necessarily mean moving to the inner city. But it does mean exposing them to costly ministry. Teach them that following Jesus, denying yourself and taking up the cross is what matters (Mark 8 v 34). And teach them that by following Jesus, denying yourself and taking up the cross for yourself.

Of course, there's nothing wrong with education, career, marriage or prosperity. But when we make these things more important than knowing and serving God, then they've become idols. The problem is they are respectable idols! It can easily become okay, even in churches, to make an idol of education or career or respectability.

Treasuring Christ

"The kingdom of heaven," says Jesus, "is like treasure hidden in a field. When a man found it, he hid it again, and then in his joy went and sold all he had and bought that field" (Matthew 13 v 44). We're not calling our children to a life of obligation and hardship that they must tough out. We're calling them to treasure! We're calling them to treasure Christ. Sacrifice there may be, but we count it joy because of the treasure that is ours in Christ. "I consider every-thing a loss," said Paul, "compared to the surpassing greatness of knowing Christ Jesus my Lord, for whose sake I have lost all things. I consider them rubbish, that I may gain Christ" (Philippians 3 v 8).

Our job is not to pressure our children into a life of begrudged duty. Our role is to extol the surpassing greatness of Christ. We're to extol Christ so much that everything else feels like rubbish in comparison.

We can't convert our children. Only the Spirit of God can open blind eyes to the truth about Jesus (John 3 v 3-8). But we can ensure our children realise what matters to us. We can communicate the surpassing value of Christ. We can teach them the importance of serving others. We can model a life lived for the glory of God. And we can pray that God will work in their hearts so that, by His grace, they see themselves first and foremost as church planters, missionaries, reformers, servants and/or evangelists.

Questions for reflection

? When your children look at your life, what do they see matters most to you?

? When your children hear you pray, what do they hear matters most to you?

? What do you praise your children for most? Passing exams? Sporting achievement? Kindness to others?

? When do your children see or hear you extolling the surpassing greatness of Christ?

? Do the things you buy for your children and the activities you provide for them teach your children to find joy in ways that distract them from enjoying God?

> ⓘ Does your life prompt your children to ask questions about God "when you sit at home and when you walk along the road' (Deuteronomy 6 v 7)?
>
> ⓘ Are you protecting your children from Christian service or preparing your children for Christian service?

Ideas for action

Think of some ways you could serve others together with your children – things like visiting an aged church member, serving coffee at church, helping someone in need.

Pray every day for the salvation of your children. And pray that they might serve Jesus with sacrificial joy. Offer them back to God for Him to send where He wills and use as He chooses.

part two

a grace-centred family

3 Disciplining a parent's heart

Principle

The biggest obstacle to good discipline is our own selfish hearts.

Consider this

"My children hate me."

Brian stirred his half-drunk coffee.

"All the other kids in church are so well behaved. It's always my lot getting into trouble. I guess people think I'm a lousy father. Spare the rod, spoil the child. That's what they say. So I try disciplining them. Try to be firm. I get really mad with them. But that only seems to make things worse. So then I cut them some slack. Go easy on them. I don't want my children to hate me. But they just take advantage. There's no respect. I want my children to respect me. It's not a big thing to ask. After all, I'm the one bank-rolling them. You should see my credit card bill."

He put his teaspoon down at last.

"What do you think?"

James paused. And then he said...

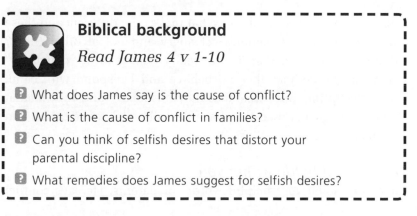

Biblical background

Read James 4 v 1-10

- [?] What does James say is the cause of conflict?
- [?] What is the cause of conflict in families?
- [?] Can you think of selfish desires that distort your parental discipline?
- [?] What remedies does James suggest for selfish desires?

Read all about it

Some true stories.

My daughter ran through the room, knocking over a chair and sending it into a glass-fronted bookcase with predictable results. "Stand still," I said calmly. "Okay, step over there and let me clear up the pieces." Our lodger stared at me, open-mouthed. "My Dad would have flown into a rage if I'd done that," she explained later. But it was an accident. And it was only a piece of furniture.

My daughter pokes at her pizza with a scowl. Some friends of mine want to meet my family so they've taken us out for a meal. But my daughter had other plans. So now my supposedly charming family can't even manage monosyllabic answers. They're not making a good impression. I'm seething inside. I am so cross. But I can't let rip. After all, we're in a restaurant. So I put on my stern voice. To no avail. Boy, are they going to get a piece of my mind when we get home.

My daughter stamps her foot in open defiance of my authority. I correct her grammar. "It's 'fewer', not 'less'."

My daughter asks me a question. Again. "How should I know where it is? Where did you last have it? Ask your mother." Two minutes later, I'm shouting. "Please just let me watch the telly in peace." Her face drops. She skulks away crest-fallen. Guilt tugs at my heart.

Which leads me to thinking. What makes the difference in these stories? Why do I sometimes get angry and not at other times? Because I've noticed that it's not really related to my daughters" behaviour. Sometimes they misbehave and I respond with calm, loving discipline. But sometimes they misbehave and I get mad at them. In fact, sometimes they haven't really misbehaved at all and I get mad at them!

Desires that battle within you

James has some very helpful words for parents. He says conflict arises from "your desires that battle within you". The problem is not my children's behaviour. The problem is my desires battling with God for control of my heart. Sure, my children misbehave. But when my heart is undivided in its allegiance to God, I respond with calm and loving discipline. But if my selfish desires are ruling my heart, then I'll respond wrongly. My discipline gets distorted by my selfishness.

Often it'll be a desire for something good. It's good to want your children to respect you. But that desire controls my heart when it matters more to me than God's glory. Here are some wrong motives for discipline:

- the desire for a quiet life
- the desire for respect or appreciation
- a fear of being embarrassed
- wanting to have our own way or be in control
- wanting your children to be "a success"

There is such a thing as right anger. God Himself is angry at sin and Jesus was angry because of His passion for God's glory. But more often than not, our anger is a sign that one of these desires (1) matters more to us than God's glory; and (2) is now being thwarted or threatened. If this selfish anger drives our discipline, the fruit will be bad. "For where you have envy and selfish ambition, there you find disorder and every evil practice" (James 3 v 16; see also Luke 6 v 43-45).

How to exasperate your children

As we saw in chapter one, the Bible tells children to obey their parents (Ephesians 6 v 1). If you're a parent, you may be rubbing your hands in glee at this point: "I can get obedient children who do whatever I want." But I mustn't make obeying me an end in itself. Obeying parents in the family is *the means* God uses to teach children to submit to His authority. The important thing is teaching our children to obey God. It's when we make ourselves the most important thing that we exasperate our children. "Fathers, do not exasperate your children; instead, bring them up in the training and instruction of the Lord" (Ephesians 6 v 4). Children are exasperated when we parent or discipline them out of selfish motives rather than out of love.

Believe me. This is the most important thing I've learnt in my years as a parent. The biggest obstacle to good discipline is my own selfish heart.

But don't despair. With God's help, you can be a good parent. Listen to 2 Peter 1 v 3-4 (with a small addition): "His divine power has given us everything we need for life and godliness [- including parenting -] through our knowledge of him who called us by his own glory and goodness. Through these he has given us his very great and precious promises, so that through them you may participate in the divine nature and escape the corruption in the world caused by evil desires."

Questions for reflection

❓ Think about the last time you got mad with your children. What did you want in that moment?

❓ Think of a time when your discipline was effective and think of a time when it was ineffective. What made the difference? What was going in your heart on each occasion?

❓ Here are some idolatrous desires that can skew your discipline. To which are you most prone? The desire for a quiet life, appreciation from your children, the respect of other people, control, success.

❓ Do you often say, "If only" when you think about your children? What comes after the "If only"? This may reveal idolatrous desires that control your heart and skew your discipline.

[?] Draw up two columns, one with the heading "selfish discipline" and the other with the heading "selfless discipline". List some contrasting characteristics of each.

[?] "Everyone should be quick to listen, slow to speak and slow to become angry, for man's anger does not bring about the righteous life that God desires" (James 1 v 19). What principles does this verse give for parenting?

[?] Look at each of these four great truths about God. How might a parent behave when they don't embrace this truth?
1. God is great – so we don't have to be in control.
2. God is glorious – so we don't have to fear others.
3. God is good – so we don't have to look elsewhere.
4. God is gracious – so we don't have to prove ourselves.

[?] Is your home parent-centred or God-centred?

4 | Grace for a parent's heart

Principle

Trying to be a good parent will crush you if you don't embrace grace.

Consider this

Here are two posts on a Christian parenting bulletin board:

It's great to be a Christian parent. And I thank God for my children that their parents are not like others – immoral, selfish and lazy. We have such a great time when we start the day with family devotions. We never miss a day – even if we're on the car-ferry or at the airport! Our home is a haven of purity. And we do so much for missions. Our children know the names of every missionary we support. We alternate learning their names with learning chapters of Romans at bed-time. Must dash. Thank you Lord! (Farah C.)

Lord, I feel useless. Please have mercy on my kids because, with a parent like me, they sure need it. (Fay Lure)

What comments would you post to each of these two statements?

Biblical background

Read Luke 18 v 9-14

- **?** Why does the Pharisee think God will approve of him?
- **?** How does the tax-collector approach God?
- **?** What does Jesus think about these two men?
- **?** How would Jesus reply to the two parenting posts above?

Read all about it

Welcome to guilt

Here's a question. Who said: "What makes you think you can write a book on parenting?" The answer is my wife. Yes, really. An unsolicited comment as she was looking over my shoulder to see what I was doing. From my "co-parent"!

I really thought my love would somehow magically produce model children. My wife planned never to give our children junk food, hoping that in later life they wouldn't like it. Can you remember the ideals you had when you were expecting your first child? They'll be there somewhere. Under a pile of dirty clothes maybe. Or drowned out by your latest row.

Parenting matters. The more we think about the responsibility of raising children, the bigger the stakes begin to look. We love our children. We want to do the best for them. But then often we get the wrong idea about what that best is, let alone putting it into practice. It's an awesome task. We want our children to get a true picture of Christian living. We don't want them to become prodigals, but neither do we want them to become Pharisees. We want people to see what a brilliant difference Christ makes to our lives. Above all, we want to please God. Gospel-centred parenting matters.

It's not surprising then that parenting often comes with guilt attached. When we get a moment to stop and think about it, we readily feel how much we've let our children down through weakness, laziness, wrong priorities and sheer selfishness. Other people's comments don't always help. "You just need to do this." "Your Jonny's a bit of handful, isn't he?" "We did it this way and never had any problems." And just when you think you've got the hang of parenting toddlers, you find they've turned into teenagers. Let's face it, you and I are pretty lousy parents. Welcome to guilt!

What we do with that guilt tells us what we really believe about the gospel. How ironic that trying to give a true picture of God's amazing forgiveness can make us feel guilty. It's more than ironic:

it can become a dangerous cycle. If we feel condemned, we won't communicate grace, making us feel still more condemned. If we want our families to be gospel-centred, then we must bring the gospel to bear on our own failures. If we can't bring our parenting sins to the cross, then we don't have any good news to celebrate. We can't communicate grace to our children if we're not communicating it to our own hearts.

Welcome to the gospel

The essence of the gospel is that God accepts us because of what Jesus did, not because of what we have done. We were God's enemies when God demonstrated His love to us on the cross (Romans 5 v 10). If He loved you when you were His enemy, then He'll love you when you lose your temper with your children. In Luke 18 it's the tax-collector who goes home accepted by God, not the Pharisee (v 14). The tax-collector knew he'd messed up. He didn't list his achievements as a parent. He simply threw himself on God's mercy. The Pharisee's long list was worth nothing. Whenever we try to earn forgiveness, we deny the grace of God. We act as if the cross was inadequate. Christ didn't do enough, we imply, to justify us before God and so we need to complete the task. Our heavenly Father commands us to confess, repent and trust His promise of forgiveness. That's how we begin the Christian life and that's how we continue in it. And that's how we continue as Christian parents.

It is liberating to discover that we are sinners. It explains why we so often rub each other up the wrong way. Put sinners together (in, say, a family!) and there'll be friction, even if they love one another. The Christian family isn't perfect. The grace of the gospel is for Christian parents too. If our parenting style reflects legalism (only rules matter) or licence (the rule of God doesn't matter), then we make it harder for our children to see and hear God's saving grace in Christ. Our children need to see how true the gospel is and how much it matters.

Welcome to grace

How are you going to handle a defiant toddler? Your child's first school detention? The evening when they stay out late? Their constant whining about household chores? You want to get it right. So much seems to hang on what you do. You'd plan what you're going to say, but your child's reactions are so unpredictable. Relax. Your intervention won't be perfect. Your motives will be mixed. Your emotions will be in turmoil. But God is gracious. He is gracious to you and He is gracious to your child. Perfection will crush you. Grace brings rest – even to the agitated parent.

Our children will only be saved by God's grace. If we're brilliant Christian parents, we can help our children see what God is really like. But they will only be born into God's family when He has mercy on them.

The parable of Farah C. and Fay Lure is a thinly-disguised version of the story of the Pharisee and the tax-collector, which Jesus told in Luke 18. Farah C. is one of those parents who intimidate the rest of us. But the cry of Fay Lure is closer to the mark: "Lord, I feel useless. Please have mercy on my kids because, with parents like us, they sure need it." Our children are greatly helped by good parenting. But they're saved by divine grace.

One of the biggest areas of guilt (or fear) for Christian parents is when their children grow up not following Jesus. The first thing to say is that we're responsible to be good witnesses to our children; we're not responsible for their salvation. God often chooses to use the witness of parents, but we can't save our children by being a good witness and neither can we thwart God's purposes by being a bad witness. Our children will answer for their own actions before God – not yours (Romans 2 v 6).

But what if you've been a bad witness? God's grace doesn't let us off the hook as parents. Our sin is still sin. It still affects our children and spoils our testimony to the reality and beauty of God's work in us. Perhaps you see your sin written into the lives of your children. It's a terrible legacy. It may yet generate a few tears. But it's not unforgiveable. Our parenting sins are addressed by God in the same way as all our sin – by grace. "If we confess our sins, he is faithful and just and will forgive us our sins and purify us from all unrighteousness" (1 John 1 v 9). And we keep on praying for our children into adulthood, praying that they will discover for themselves the liberating grace of God.

Questions for reflection

▣ Can you remember the ideals you had when you were expecting your first child?

▣ Here's what the Bible doesn't say about parenting: *"We show everyone what good Christians we are by having lovely children. The more we do this, the more accepted by God we feel. If we're good parents, then we'll know God's blessing and have a good standing in other people's eyes. Then we can feel really good about ourselves."* Does any of this sound familiar? Compare it with what the Bible really says in Romans 5 v 1-2.

▣ What do you feel guilty about as a parent?

▣ How do your children see you deal with sin and failure? How does it reflect the gospel?

▣ Over what parenting issues do you need to repent? Over what parenting issues do you need to trust the grace of God?

5 Disciplining a child's heart

Principle

Addressing the heart matters more than
controlling behaviour.

Consider this

Daniel slammed the door. "Oh, I'll just leave him," his
mother said. "It's because he's tired."

Daniel slammed the door. "Come down here at once," shouted
his mother. "Otherwise I'll give you what for. I slave away doing
your cleaning, cooking, washing, and I've only asked you to do
one, small thing. You never think about me. Your sister's been very
helpful today. Why can't you be like her? Listen, if you do as I've
asked, I'll give you some money to go the cinema this evening."

Daniel slammed the door. His mother sighed. "Think calm
thoughts," she muttered. Up she went. She knocked on his door.
"Whhhaaaaat?"

"Your reaction then was well out of order. What made you so
angry? What's going on?"

Biblical background

Read Colossians 2 v 20 – 3 v 10

- ❓ What does a set of rules appear to produce in someone's life?
- ❓ What does a set of rules actually produce in someone's life?
- ❓ How do we get rid of wrong behaviour?

Read all about it

Why do children misbehave?

Children can be naïve, gullible, vulnerable. That's why they need protecting. But they're not innocent. "Surely I was sinful at birth, sinful from the time my mother conceived me" (Psalm 51 v 5).

So why do children misbehave? Here are some options:

- "It's because he's tired."
- "It's the other girls at school – they lead her astray."
- "She just gets a bit hyper."
- "His hormones are going crazy."
- "Too many video games."
- "It's all the additives they put in children's food."
- "It's just the way he is."
- "He's just hungry."
- "He's misunderstood."
- "ADHD." (Attention Deficit Hyperactivity Disorder)
- "I blame the parents."

These may all be contributing factors. But they don't get to the heart of the matter.

What does Jesus say? "From within, out of men's hearts, come evil thoughts, sexual immorality, theft, murder, adultery, greed, malice, deceit, lewdness, envy, slander, arrogance and folly. All these evils come from inside and make a man 'unclean'" (Mark 7 v 21-23).

Evil behaviour comes from within, from our hearts. Children misbehave because they have sinful, selfish hearts.

The source of all actions – both good and bad – is the heart. And that means changing hearts matters more than controlling behaviour.

Paul says living by a set of rules can appear impressive (Colossians 2 v 20-23). Rules can appear to change behaviour. But they don't produce lasting results. They can't control sensual indulgence.

From controlling behaviour...

In chapter three we saw that the biggest obstacle to good discipline is our own selfish heart. And wrong motives lead to wrong ways of disciplining. If your aim is selfish (for a quiet life, for example, or your reputation), then you'll do whatever it takes to control your child's *behaviour*. Here are some examples:

- Manipulation ("Your sister did it okay.")
- Fear ("You won't know what's hit you.")
- Bribery ("I'll give you a sweet if you shut up.")
- Emotionalism ("After all I've done for you.")
- Inconsistency ("Okay, just this once.")

...to addressing the heart

But if your aim is to teach your child the ways of God, then your discipline will be calm, clear, consistent and concentrated on the motives of their heart. The goal is not control – that's *your* agenda. God's agenda is a child who delights to know and serve Him.

Ephesians 4 v 22 talks about "deceitful desires". Our hearts always desire, treasure, want and worship. Sinful behaviour arises when our hearts treasure something more than God. We're deceived into thinking it offers more than knowing and serving God. It might be a desire for something that in itself is good, like the approval of friends. But when that matters more than the approval of God, it's become a deceitful or idolatrous desire. The sign of this is that it bears bad fruit in our lives (Luke 6 v 43-45). The desire for the approval of friends, for example, might cause a child to slam the door when you say "no" to the latest fashion gear, or to shop-lift in order to impress friends.

So good discipline is:

1. Calm

The focus of discipline is the child's heart rather than your emotional state. More often than not, we get angry because we're not getting the respect, quiet or control we want. That's not a good place from which to exercise discipline.

2. Clear

Make your commands clear. It took me ages to realise it, but "calm down" is a useless command. A child doesn't know what it looks like in practice. Tell a child clearly what you want. A good test is: will it be clear if they are disobeying your command? We found counting to five a helpful way of making it clear that our children had to obey now. One, two, three… By five they had to act or face discipline. (In public I would sometimes raise my fingers one at a time so no one else knew what was happening.)

And make your discipline clear. Ensure your child links your discipline with their wrong behaviour. Explain why they're being disciplined. With very young children that means discipline must be immediate.

3. Consistent

First, set consistent boundaries. Obviously boundaries change as children grow older, but don't discipline today what you allowed yesterday. Inconsistent boundaries encourage children to challenge your authority.

Second, always follow through with warnings. "You'll go to your room if you do that again" must lead to a child being sent to their room if they do. (It also means no empty threats like "You'll never watch telly again".)

Third, be consistent between parents. Children often try to play off one parent against another. If one parent says "No", they'll ask the other. So get in the habit of saying things like: "Yes, as long as that's okay with your mother."

4. Concentrated on the heart

The most important thing about good discipline is that it's concentrated on the heart.

What does this mean in practice?

- Focus on the motivation of your child, not just their behaviour. "What did you want?" "What were you hoping to achieve?" "Why did you do it?" "What matters most to you?" "Help me understand what you were thinking."
- Listen hard to understand your children. Why are they frustrated, miserable or angry? What do they want that they're not getting?
- Cut through the mire of "she said, he said, she started it, he started it" with a focus on the heart. "I don't care who started it. You both got angry because you wanted your own way."
- Move away from "boundary discussions" ("How far can I go?") to the centre – the spirit of love ("What's the loving thing to do?").
- Realise that the child who sulks in their room is behaving as badly as the child who shouts at you. The sulking child may suit your agenda (for control or comfort), but they're expressing their selfishness just as much as the shouting child.
- Lead your child to Christ. We can change our behaviour – at least a bit for a while. But we need a Saviour to change our hearts. Acknowledge what you're asking is hard for your child. "We need God's help. How about we pray?" Godly discipline highlights for a child their need of Christ.

Ideas for action

Here are some ideas for discipline (what you do will vary depending on the age and personality of your child):

- Expressions of disapproval (a stern talking to, the naughty step).
- A calm smack preceded by an explanation and followed by a cuddle.
- Isolation (sending them to their room, grounding them).
- Letting children face the natural consequences of their actions (let them be late for school, don't replace toys they've carelessly broken).
- Removing privileges (because privileges go together with responsibilities).

With younger children the aim of discipline is to teach them to submit to authority. So when you give choices, make sure you set the options your child can choose from. "Do you want to wear your coat, or take it with you in a bag?" "Which piece of fruit do you want?" With completely open questions like: "Wouldn't it be better if you came in now?" your child becomes the decision-maker and your authority is reduced to negotiation.

As children grow older, however, you should move your child from discipline to self-discipline, ready for when they leave your authority. So involve them more in setting boundaries and consequences. Allow discussion and debate as long as it remains respectful. Help them see that privileges go together with responsibilities.

"Discipline your son, and he will give you peace; he will bring delight to your soul" (Proverbs 29 v 17).

Questions for reflection

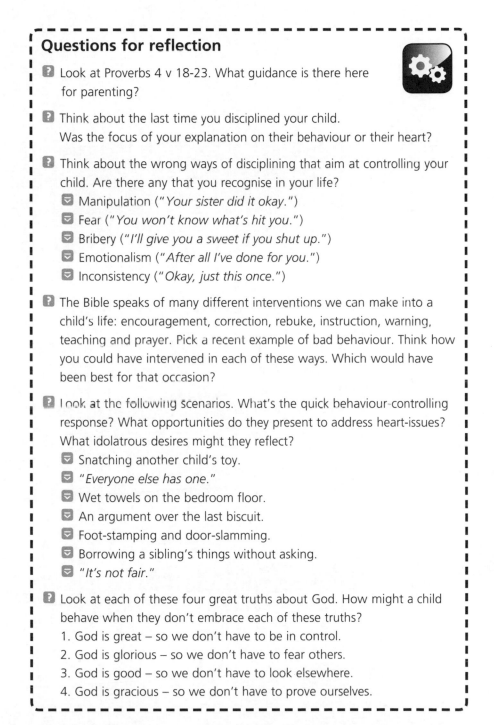

[?] Look at Proverbs 4 v 18-23. What guidance is there here for parenting?

[?] Think about the last time you disciplined your child. Was the focus of your explanation on their behaviour or their heart?

[?] Think about the wrong ways of disciplining that aim at controlling your child. Are there any that you recognise in your life?
- Manipulation (*"Your sister did it okay."*)
- Fear (*"You won't know what's hit you."*)
- Bribery (*"I'll give you a sweet if you shut up."*)
- Emotionalism (*"After all I've done for you."*)
- Inconsistency (*"Okay, just this once."*)

[?] The Bible speaks of many different interventions we can make into a child's life: encouragement, correction, rebuke, instruction, warning, teaching and prayer. Pick a recent example of bad behaviour. Think how you could have intervened in each of these ways. Which would have been best for that occasion?

[?] Look at the following scenarios. What's the quick behaviour-controlling response? What opportunities do they present to address heart-issues? What idolatrous desires might they reflect?
- Snatching another child's toy.
- *"Everyone else has one."*
- Wet towels on the bedroom floor.
- An argument over the last biscuit.
- Foot-stamping and door-slamming.
- Borrowing a sibling's things without asking.
- *"It's not fair."*

[?] Look at each of these four great truths about God. How might a child behave when they don't embrace each of these truths?
1. God is great – so we don't have to be in control.
2. God is glorious – so we don't have to fear others.
3. God is good – so we don't have to look elsewhere.
4. God is gracious – so we don't have to prove ourselves.

6 Grace for a child's heart

Principle

Don't train your child to be a legalist.

Consider this

"Can you wash up, please?"

"Do I have to? I did it yesterday. What about Theo? He's not doing anything. It's not fair."

"Please do as you're told. If you do it now, then I'll let you have half-an-hour on your games console thingy."

"Half-an-hour? It's got to be worth more than that. How about an hour?"

"Okay, an hour then. But make sure you leave the kitchen tidy."

Some time later.

"The washing up's not been done! I told you to do it. I can't believe it. It's one thing after another. I don't know why I bother. You're such a waste of space. No, it's too late now. Just go away. Leave me alone. Go on. Out of my sight."

Biblical background

Read Luke 15 v 11-32

❓ What does the attitude of the father reveal about the attitude of God?

❓ What does the attitude of the older brother reveal about the attitude of many of us?

❓ What kind of a parent would the older brother be?

❓ Look at all the things the older brother says. Turn them into something a parent might say to their children.

Read all about it

We're natural-born legalists. A legalist is someone who tries to make the grade by doing the right things. These days people have all sorts of ideas about what "making it" involves. Some people want to prove themselves by making it to the top; others to be worshipped by the opposite sex. Religious legalists want to get right with God through religious activity or moral behaviour. It's pride – we want to claim the credit for who we are.

Children are not immune. "Look what I've done." "I've done it better than Ed." "Will you let me go round to Jane's if I wash up." "It's not fair," they cry when they don't get what they think they deserve, and "It's not fair," they cry when someone else gets more than they think they deserve.

They echo the attitude of the older brother in Luke 15. "All these years I've slaved for you. Never disobeyed. And what do I get? Look at what he's done. And you love him more!" He sees himself as a slave, not a son. He's trying to earn his father's affection when he doesn't need to. "My son," the father said, "you are always with me, and everything I have is yours."

The challenge for parenting is that, if we're not careful, our discipline can reinforce this innate legalism. Our children learn that good behaviour earns acceptance while bad behaviour earns rejection. In the last chapter we looked at the importance of influencing our child's heart rather than controlling their behaviour. The reality is that we're always influencing our child's heart even when we're trying to control their behaviour. The question is: *How* are we influencing their heart? Could it be we're training our children to be legalists? Could we be teaching them that changing behaviour earns acceptance?

So we need to communicate grace to our children.

That doesn't mean no discipline at all. That's not how grace works with God. Grace takes sin very seriously – much more seriously than legalism (which thinks we can overcome sin through our own effort) or license (which thinks sin doesn't matter very much). Grace says sin matters so much that Jesus had to die in our place. "The Lord disciplines those he loves" (Hebrews 12 v 6). God accepts us as we are by grace, but He accepts us with an agenda of change. Of course He does: He wants the best for us, which is to become like His Son.

It's the same with parenting. Grace doesn't mean no discipline. Instead, it changes the *way* we discipline. We combine discipline with love and acceptance. We discipline our children and point to the forgiveness won on the cross. We accept our children as they are, but with an agenda for change.

What does this mean in practice?

1. **Discipline and then stop.** Don't harbour a grudge. Don't make them feel as if they've got to earn your love or get back in your good books.

2. **Always show acceptance to your child when you've disciplined them.** There should be no hint of rejection. Discipline and then cuddle (or whatever the equivalent is for your teenager). Never humiliate your child. As far as possible, praise them in public and discipline them in private.

3. **Once again we see how important it is to discipline our own hearts.** If I discipline out of selfish anger, then I'll probably carry on being grumpy with my children. I'll communicate that you need to behave right if you want my affection. We should always discipline as an act of love, not retaliation.

4. **Don't use bribery to control your children.** Bribery's another word for legalism. Teach children to do the right thing because it's the right thing – not because of any unrelated reward. Bribery motivates children to get the reward rather than do the right thing. Take the reward away and the motivation is gone.

It also makes behaviour negotiable. The true reward for doing the right thing is that it pleases Mummy and Daddy – and, ultimately, that it pleases God. The reward awaiting God's children is God Himself.

5. **Make sure your child knows you discipline them because you love them.** You're not trying to make them into someone you'll find loveable.

6. **Legalism looks down on other people because that makes you feel good about yourself.** Do your children hear you putting other people down? Do you view others with self-righteous pride?

7. **Don't compare your child to other children.** "Why can't you be like Jonny?" "At least you're not as bad as Susie." "Did you get a better grade than your friends?"

8. **Say sorry to your children when you don't get it right.** Don't pretend to be perfect. Let them know that you're a sinner in need of God's grace.

9. **Above all, bring your children to the cross.** Teach them about the cross. Extol the cross. Thank God with them for the cross. Sing about the cross.

Questions for reflection

❓ Think of some parents you admire. What makes them great parents?

❓ Take a look at the following paragraph. I've taken some verses from the Bible and made them say the opposite of what they actually say. See if you can turn them back into what they really say. You can check by looking at Titus 3 v 5-8.
We are saved by God's mercy plus the righteous things we do. We get rid of our sins and start on a new life with help from the Holy Spirit, whom God generously gives us from time to time through Jesus Christ our Saviour. This is how we can prove ourselves and can have confidence that we will have eternal life. This is a trustworthy saying, and I want you to stress this teaching so that everyone will devote themselves to doing what is good.

❓ What tendencies towards legalism can you detect in your own life?

❓ When was the last time you said sorry to your children?

❓ When was the last time you talked about the cross with your children? What opportunities can you think of to talk about the cross with your children?

❓ What struggles are your children facing at the moment? What opportunities do these struggles offer for your child's spiritual development? What could you do to help them grow in this area?

7 Children as a gift

Make sure you enjoy your children.

Consider this

Omar was late leaving the office again. It was standing room only on the train. At Wimbledon a load of people got out so he finally sat down and got out his book on parenting. Ah, parenting. It was so confusing. Corporate deals, annual reviews, product development all seemed so straight-forward compared to getting it right with his children.

When he got home, he could sense his wife had had enough. So he took charge as best he could. Dinner. Check. (Important to ensure their nutritional needs were met.) Washing up. Check. (Important to ensure they learnt to serve.) Homework. Check. (Important to ensure they did well at school.) Teeth. Check. (Important to ensure they were healthy.) Bible and prayer. Check. (Important to ensure they learnt about God.) Bed. Check.

He poured himself a drink. Parenting. Check. Maybe he could manage it after all. Was there anything else, he wondered, that should go on his new parenting checklist?

Biblical background

Read Psalm 127

❓ Is a successful family simply a question of hard work?

❓ What truths in this psalm will stop you lying awake at night worrying about your family?

❓ What does the psalm say are the blessings that children bring?

❓ Solomon, the author of this psalm, built a house (= temple) for the Lord. But he realised the future depended on the Lord's promise of a house (= dynasty) to his father David (2 Samuel 7). What hope does Jesus, the Son of David, bring to your family situation?

Read all about it

What are your happiest childhood memories? Here are some of mine. Dens in the wood. Play fighting. Cricket in the garden. Science projects on the windowsill. Damming streams. Mum finding we'd smashed a picture playing with a balloon and then discovering Dad was the culprit. Turning the front room into a camp. Trips out, yes, though usually the trips that went wrong. Like when the car broke down and we built a camp by the side of the road. Except you don't always know whether you really remember it or whether you just remember the many times the story's been retold round the meal table.

Children are a gift from the Lord. There are times when they can seem a strange gift. A Great-Aunt's-Christmas-hand-knitted-orange-woolly-sweater sort of a gift. Sometimes they can even feel more like a curse. When they wake you for the fourth time in the night. When they throw up all over you. When they slam the door in your face. When you get your credit card bill. But a gift they are.

In the midst of trying hard to be a good parent, don't forget to receive the gift with thanks. And enjoy it. And think, too, how you can help your children enjoy their family life.

1. *Showing love*

   Your first responsibility as a parent is to love your child. Love is often unseen, serving them behind the scenes. Often it's unnoticed. The clean clothes are taken for granted. But also ensure your children know you love them. Be affectionate. Tell them you love them. Always say good night. (A good relationship is also the foundation of good discipline because then your approval and disapproval matter to your children.)

2. *Spending time*

   Relationships take time. There's no way round it. Don't believe all that stuff about "quality-time". With children, quality-time requires quantity-time. Don't buy your children's affection by giving them lots of presents. There's no substitute for spending time with them. Sometimes you can involve them in what you're doing. At other times let them set the agenda. You may not be fascinated by beetles or dinosaurs or R'n'B or football, but let their enthusiasm rub off on you.

3. *Being available*

   Fix events that are important to your children in your diary (birthdays, school concerts). As they get older they become less keen on hanging out with Mum and Dad. But try to be available for them. There'll be times when they want to talk. Often inconvenient times. But do your best to be available. Our girls never want to talk about their school day when they first get home. There's no point pushing them. But often it all comes out later in the evening.

4. *Talking together*

Communication is at the heart of relationships. Your children won't talk about deep, personal stuff with you, if you haven't first talked about a load of trivial stuff. Listen to them. Really listen to them. Put your book down. Switch off the television. Turn away from your computer. Listen to the words and listen to what's underlying the words.

5. *Pursuing conversation*

Try to have a daily conversation with each of your children. Not instructions. Not rebukes. Not talk over the telly. Conversation. If they're reluctant, don't command it of them. Think of it as an investment in your relationship, in which you patiently pursue them every day as far as they'll go. When you're away from home, write a letter or send a postcard.

6. *Eating together*

Think how important meals were in the ministry of Jesus. That's because meals are talking times, bonding times, community times. They express and reinforce relation-ships. So try to eat together at least once a day (with the TV off). Play games over the meal table. "Would you rather…?" "Tell us one thing you learned today…" "Words that rhyme with…"

7. *Creating together*

Be creative with your children. Make Christmas cards. Read to them. Build Lego castles. Bake cakes. Start a shared hobby – it might become something you do together for the rest of your life.

8. *Playing games*

Play with your children. Kick a football in the park. Pretend to be pirates, sailing on the sofa. Try to make each other say "yes" or "no". Board games. (Remember to let them win sometimes.) Get on your hands and knees with your children. My Dad amused us for hours by "magically" throwing his slipper through the mirror and making it reappear in different places round the house. (He'd hide the left slipper; then, as he pretended to throw the right slipper, he'd drop it behind his back. As we ran off to look for one slipper, he'd hide the other ready for next time.)

9. *Creating memories*
   Every now and then, plan to create a memory for your children – something they'll look back on affectionately in years to come. Growing sunflowers. A treasure hunt. Sleeping in a home-made den. Restoring an old motorbike. Go for something that involves thought and preparation rather than just paying for a trip out.

10. *Telling stories*
    One of the things that binds families together is their shared stories. "Do you remember when...?"

We don't always view our children as a gift. They can sometimes feel more like work than pleasure! Especially when a child has a disability or illness, we need to fight the temptation to become bitter. More often, though, I observe parents viewing their disabled or sick child as a special gift from God, albeit one wrapped up with struggle and heartache.

Children are sometimes a gift that God takes away. I know a father embittered for a lifetime because his son died of a heart condition aged eleven. When Job lost his ten children in one day he was able to say: "The LORD gave and the LORD has taken away; may the name of the LORD be praised" (Job 1 v 21).

Questions for reflection

Think of times when your children have:
- made you laugh
- made you proud
- filled you with joy
- moved you to tears

Ask your children about their happy family memories.

What were your family traditions when you were growing up? What are your family traditions now? Could you create a new tradition?

When did you last take time to find out what your child was thinking? What did you discover?

"The best way to get my Dad's attention was to do be naughty." Could that be said of you?

"If your child is ten years old, 3,650 days have already gone. You have 2,920 left." (Rob Parsons) Does this encourage you to make any changes? What's your plan?

Ideas for action

Take photos of your children, but also keep a box with their drawings, certificates, school projects and so on. And keep a book in which you write down the funny things they say (useful when it comes to the father-of-the-bride speech).

Thank God for your children. List specific things about your children that give you cause for thanksgiving.

a word-centred family

8 Living the word

Principle

Teach your children about God in the context of everyday life.

Consider this

Joanna smiled as she watched Ben and Sophie, her two youngest children, at play. "They chat so happily in their "let's pretend" games," she thought. It was frightening how accurate their take was on how Joanna's friends treated each other. Yesterday's game was called "helping hands" and involved taking pies round to friends who were housebound. Last week's "speed cops" had been inspired by Dad's encounter with a policeman, a radar and a speeding ticket!

"If this is how Ben and Sophie see our lives," Joanna wondered, "what do they make of our Christian faith?"

Biblical background

Read Deuteronomy 11 v 16-21

? How are we to keep ourselves from idols?

? How can we parents keep our children from idols?

? What's the principle behind the command to tie the Lord's commands on the forehead, hand and doorpost?

? Read Deuteronomy 6 v 4-25. How many different settings are mentioned for learning God's word in Deuteronomy 6 v 4-9 and 11 v 16-21?

? Look at Deuteronomy 6 v 20-25. What message should we be passing on in these situations? What is the New Testament version of this story?

Read all about it

How come my children know so much about driving? Sometimes my sons are anxious about my speed and my use of indicators. At other times they demand to know why we've not overtaken the white van ahead. Where do they get it from? After all, children don't take driving lessons.

The answer, of course, is that, for my sons, being driven in a car is part of their everyday experience. Like all children, they pick up on what's going on around them. They analyse everything they see and hear. So they've learned about driving by watching their parents' everyday driving.

Driving is a great parable of our role as Christian parents. We get on with the business of life. We work. We play. We watch telly. We help others. We sulk. We laugh. We grumble. We praise. We fall out and make up. We spend money. We talk about decisions. And all the time our children are watching, listening and learning.

We take our children to church, read the Bible with them and pray together. But this is only a fraction of what we teach our children. They watch our every move. Listen to your children playing and you'll hear yourself echoing back. Your everyday talk teaches them what you really care about. Your everyday talk teaches them how you love God. John Younts says: "Your everyday talk reveals where your treasure is, and therefore where your heart is."

We keep the Lord at the centre of our homes by keeping Him at the centre of our hearts. And we keep Him in our hearts by fixing His word in our hearts. As we do this, we keep ourselves from idols. Deuteronomy tells us that we are to express our love for the Lord in our everyday actions and to declare His word in our everyday talk (6 v 4-9; 11 v 18-25).

Bible time

As Christian parents, we're to fix God's words in our own hearts and teach them to our children (Deuteronomy 11 v 18-19). That means we need to be reading the Bible for ourselves – and letting our children know we do this (without an ostentatious "quiet time").

It also means spending time reading the Bible and praying with our children. A little each day is always better than a lot once in a while. Adapt as family life changes. Sometimes reading at bedtime works best; sometimes at breakfast.

This is your job as a parent. Your church and its youth groups may be partners in this. But we shouldn't "out-source" the responsibility to them. We are the ones who are with them every day and the ones to whom God has entrusted them.

Everyday talk

Teaching goes on long after Bible time finishes. It happens when we sit at home, when we walk along the road, when we lie down, and when we get up. It even happens when a six-year-old jumps on top of us.

This doesn't mean a sermon at breakfast. It needn't mean Bible verses scrawled on the fridge door. It means that we show our love for God's word by the way our whole family life happens. It means the word of God is close to the surface of every conversation. It means every topic has the potential to include God. Here are three areas where we can make a start.

First, think about how you talk to your spouse and about your spouse. Does the way you talk to your spouse communicate respect, love and grace? "Your father's such a waste of space." "Don't listen to your mother, she doesn't know what she's talking about." "Marriage is a ball and chain, son." Marriage is a picture of Christ's relationship to the church (Ephesians 5 v 22-33). Children learn about the liberating lordship of Jesus when they see their mother putting her husband's will before her own. They learn how Christ loves the church when they see their father serving their mother after he's had a hard day at work. Your children will listen to your angry silences as well. They may well end up thinking that we must atone for our sin before forgiveness can be given. But surely it's the gospel of grace that you want to teach your children.

You have an opportunity to do so every time you interact with your spouse.

Second, think about how you talk about suffering, failure and crises. This is often when our real beliefs surface. Grumbling, self-pity, anger, bitterness, frustration. What do these communicate about our willingness to submit to the lordship of Jesus? Life doesn't have to be going well for good parenting to take place: the ups and downs of family life can give us opportunities to model godly responses. Our instinct is often to protect our children from difficulties. But how we apply the gospel to illness, bereavement, unemployment and conflict can demonstrate what it means for God to be our strong tower. It can show that Christ is worth more than life itself. It can show that treasure in heaven matters more than treasure on earth.

Third, think about celebrations and festivals – Easter, Christmas, family birthdays and anniversaries. Celebrations are a great time to have fun and create good memories of family life together. But what we celebrate will also be a learning opportunity. Too often, Christmas celebrates possessions more than Jesus, with the shopping catalogue as our sacred text rather than the Bible. The world, rather than the word, sets the agenda. For God's people, festivals should teach us afresh the story of God's salvation. When Moses gave instructions on how to keep the Passover, it was so that parents could explain God's rescue to their children (Exodus 13 v 14-16).

You may not be a good reader or see yourself as a Bible teacher. But if you're a Christian, then you have the best teacher of all at hand – the Holy Spirit. Some of your children's questions may stump you (they've been the trickiest theological questions I've had to answer). But don't underestimate the power of the word lived and the word loved.

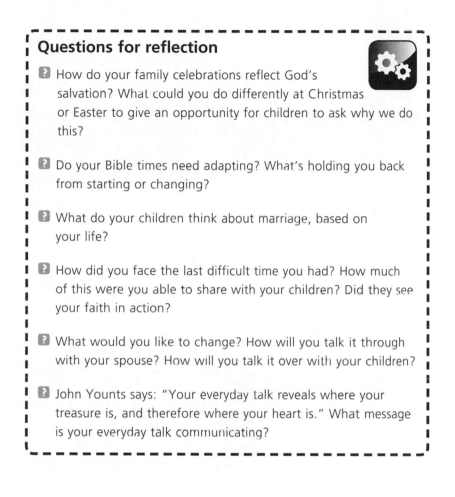

Questions for reflection

🔹 How do your family celebrations reflect God's salvation? What could you do differently at Christmas or Easter to give an opportunity for children to ask why we do this?

🔹 Do your Bible times need adapting? What's holding you back from starting or changing?

🔹 What do your children think about marriage, based on your life?

🔹 How did you face the last difficult time you had? How much of this were you able to share with your children? Did they see your faith in action?

🔹 What would you like to change? How will you talk it through with your spouse? How will you talk it over with your children?

🔹 John Younts says: "Your everyday talk reveals where your treasure is, and therefore where your heart is." What message is your everyday talk communicating?

9 The word and other voices

Principle

Shape WHAT younger children watch and HOW older children watch.

Consider this

In between rounds of trivia questions, Phil asked his pub quiz team: "If your family were a building, what would it be?"

Nigel's was a **fortress**: "My role is to protect my children from the world, making sure the drawbridge is kept up."

Jack drew a stage: "We're training the next generation of celebrities!"

Jonah had a **camper van** with himself at the wheel. "Life's an adventure," he said. "I want my kids to explore and enjoy everything life has to offer."

Monty was in his **greenhouse**. "This is where we grow and toughen tender plants, ready for the time when they will have to fend for themselves."

Stephen said: "A **factory**. My children are going to be high-achievers and I need to make sure that they're prepared in the best way possible – good food, education, experiences and friends are essential for top performance."

The next round of quiz questions started and they all spent ten minutes trying to remember the capital city of Vanuatu.

Then someone piped up: "Hang on a minute. What about you, Phil? How do you see your family?"

Read all about it

"You can take a man out of the world, but you cannot take the world out of a man." That's why, according to the Reformer Martin Luther, monasteries will never be free from sin. They might be cut off from the world's influence, but sin resides in the human heart.

Families might seem a long way from monastic life. They don't offer the same level of peace and tranquillity. Plus vows of chastity aren't a good basis for building a family! But we share a similar desire to protect ourselves from the temptations of the world. But if taking ourselves out of the world is ineffective, what can we do?

It's important to recognise that the world around us has always contained siren voices that want to seduce us. Proverbs warns of the sinful woman whose smooth tongue lures fools into sin. The wise parent will prepare their child to resist this call (6 v 23-24).

There are many voices today calling to our children: TV, books, magazines, the internet, friends and school can all be mouthpieces for the "sinful woman" described in Proverbs, enticing our children away from what's right. We can't isolate them for ever, so how can we prepare them?

Shape what YOU watch and how YOU watch

The first step is to decide how YOU are going to engage with the world. Christians will come to different decisions, but be sure you're clear on your rationale because your children will test your boundaries. They'll want to know why you've drawn the boundary *here* and not *there*. If you're unclear where *you* stand, you'll soon feel threatened and defensive. And that'll lead to knee-jerk responses rather than a thought-through, gospel-centred approach.

Guard your own heart (Philippians 4 v 8). Ask: "What is this film, book, programme, website filling my mind with?" We're all susceptible to different temptations so your boundaries may differ from those of other people. What thoughts and fantasies does this suggest to me? Does it help me fulfil my God-given responsibilities? Does this romantic comedy or makeover show make me dissatisfied?

Don't simply judge what you watch by how graphic or explicit it is. An innocent-looking sitcom may be more insidious than a graphic film that shows the destructive nature of sin, because the sitcom undermines our sense of what is appropriate by its slow drip of assumptions about what constitutes normal behaviour. Don't switch your brain off: reflecting biblically on what we watch will enable us to appreciate the God-given creativity in our culture, without succumbing to its sin-induced corrosion.

Shape WHAT younger children watch

With younger children, Nigel's picture of the family as a fortress is appropriate. Make good use of the off switch – then children will learn that TV-on is not the default position. It's a good idea to watch *with* children rather than use the TV as a free baby-sitter. As they grow older, talk with them about what you're watching – even if that means, as it does for me, a lot of time discussing *Batman*. Some children cope better with scary stories than others. They can be a great opportunity to talk about the protective care of our heavenly Father and to model that in a bedtime prayer. When tensions arise, be prepared to explain your decisions so that children learn for themselves the why, when and what of TV watching.

Christian families will come to different conclusions on, say, the latest teenage wizard books and films. But be supportive of decisions other families make, treating one another as those whose conscience is weaker – or stronger (Romans 15 v 1). Stick to their rules when their children are with you.

Shape HOW older children watch

As they grow older, children spend less time under your supervision. So it's not enough to regulate what they watch. The fortress needs to become a greenhouse in which plants are toughened up for life outside. So we need to train children to engage with films and books in the same way that we do. Talk about what they're watching. "What did you like and why?" "How realistic was it?" "What message did it convey?" Ask about aspects that don't fit biblical values. Films often connect with questions people are asking, so explore those connections together and identify biblical answers.

"Everyone else watches it," our girls would often exclaim. We soon learned "everyone" might mean one or two of their friends. But part of discussing with teenagers is explaining why you've put the boundaries *there*. One day your children will be free to do whatever they want. Your aim as a trainer is to prepare them to make good decisions for themselves.

> *"Listen, my sons, to a father's instruction;*
> *pay attention and gain understanding.*
> *I give you sound learning,*
> *so do not forsake my teaching" (Proverbs 4 v 1-2).*

Questions for reflection

❓ Talk to your children about their favourite programmes. Which programmes do they like? Why do they like them?

❓ Keep a record of your children's television watching. What does it reveal?

❓ What limits do you put on your children's TV and film watching? What reasons can you give for putting the limits there?

❓ How will you respond to the fact that another family lets their children watch things you don't? What if that family are Christians?

❓ What has helped you think about the films you watch and the books you read? How can you teach your children to think in the same way?

❓ When do your children hear the voice of God? When do your children hear the voice of the world? Whose voice do they hear most?

Ideas for action

Make some television programmes into eagerly antici-pated family events. My teenage girls still make sure they're in to watch *Dr Who* together as a family.

Teach your children to watch adverts critically. Ask them what the advert promised ("a new you") and what the product will actually deliver ("clean hair"). We sometimes play "guess the product". It's either a race to recognise the advert or a guess at the product if it's a new advert. It's a fun use of the ad break, but also highlights how unrealistic the promises and images of advertising are, and how unrelated to the actual products.

10 Praying the word

Principle

Teach children to pray by praying with them.

Consider this

"Dear God, thank You for looking after us today. Please bless mummy and baby Flo. And please look after all the children in poor countries. Amen."

"Amen," repeated Craig. "Love you, Dad."

It wasn't often Brian got to pray with his son, what with working late or rushing out for church events. Praying together was good. He wanted his son to see his relationship with God was real. Yet he also felt uneasy. What kind of reality was he communicating? Truth was, sometimes his relationship with God seemed a little unreal. How could he teach his son to pray when his own prayer life was so perfunctory? Perhaps he should do something to spice up his own praying.

When he asked Doug if he had any suggestions, Doug said...

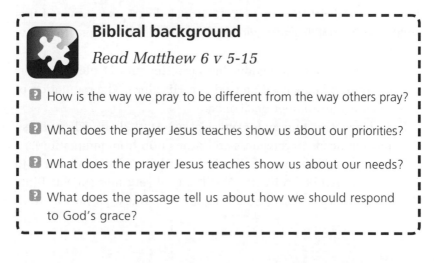

Biblical background

Read Matthew 6 v 5-15

❓ How is the way we pray to be different from the way others pray?

❓ What does the prayer Jesus teaches show us about our priorities?

❓ What does the prayer Jesus teaches show us about our needs?

❓ What does the passage tell us about how we should respond to God's grace?

Read all about it

You can tell a lot about a Christian's relationship with God from the way they pray. So teaching our children to pray is not about imparting a procedure, but teaching them the character of God and His gospel. We're teaching them how to relate to God.

Learn from your children how to pray

There's a strong temptation for Christians to think of prayer as a technique; to want to become "advanced" pray-ers; to make spirituality an achievement on our part. But the achievement of prayer is all God's. What makes prayer "successful" is the gospel – the blood of Christ bringing us into the presence of God. The dominant biblical image of a pray-er is that of a child petitioning its father. If we want a gospel-centred family, then we may need to learn gospel-centredness from our children. Think about how your children ask you for things. They don't confine themselves to special times or places. They don't construct eloquent little speeches. They come with confidence, secure in your love and dependent on your care.

This is how Jesus teaches us to pray – to pray to a heavenly Father (Matthew 6 v 9-13).

We call God "Father" because He adopts us into His family when we come to Christ (Romans 8 v 15-16). He hears us because of this relationship, not because we use lots of clever words (Matthew 6 v 7-8).

We pray for God's kingdom because His rule is blessing. Our prayers should be focused on God and His glory. The reputation of His name is our number one concern.

Jesus teaches us to pray for physical needs (daily bread), but also for spiritual needs (forgiveness and protection from temptation).

Prayer is a natural part of the Christian life and so we want it to be a natural part of family life. We'll pray at set times such as Bible time, meal times and at the start of journeys. But we'll pray as well when anything special occurs, such as hearing good or sad news. Your children don't wait for a special time before they talk to you!

The Bible encourages us to ask specifically. "Do not be anxious about anything, but in everything, by prayer and petition ... present your requests to God." (Philippians 4 v 6) Let's train our children to ask and to expect God to answer. Talk about answers to prayer. Pray for safe travel at the beginning of journeys, for example, but also give thanks for safe arrival at the end of journeys. Don't be afraid of unanswered prayers – they're an opportunity to talk about God's sovereignty, wisdom and purposes.

Pray with gospel priorities

Our prayers reveal our true concerns and young children's prayers can be quite random. We started by asking them to thank God for something. They praised God for the lampshade! (We did have to step in when they addressed the milk bottle: it is *God* whom we thank for our food!) We moved on to encourage our children to thank God for always keeping His promises.

Encourage them to bring their concerns, however random, to their heavenly Father. We don't want them to think some topics are off-limits in prayer. But we also want the gospel to shape their concerns, giving them God-centred priorities. One of the main ways we teach these priorities is in the way we ourselves pray. Pray with your children for their immediate concerns, but also pray for their relationship with God and their service of Him.

Remember there is a world beyond the front door. "Hallowed be your name, your kingdom come, your will be done." We need to pray as a family for world events, mission partners, and for other children throughout the world. Be creative: use photos, stories or what they've been watching on television to help children relate to distant prayer issues.

Pray as a whole family, even if it's brief. Mealtimes and journeys (with everyone strapped in!) are natural times to pray together. Pray, too, with individual children. Paul seems to have this model of personal attention in mind when he says: "Know that we dealt with each of you as a father deals with his own children, encouraging, comforting and urging you to live lives worthy of God, who calls you into his kingdom and glory" (1 Thessalonians 2 v 11-12). If you're the only Christian parent in the family, your spouse may be unwilling for you to pray with the whole family. But you may still be able to pray *with* your children and you can always pray *for* them and for your spouse.

Praying out loud with other people can be scary. We are exposed because our relationship with God is on show. But for parents this is a great opportunity. We want our children to see how we relate to God so that they will learn to do the same.

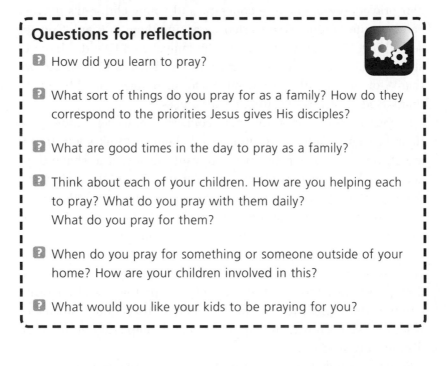

Questions for reflection

? How did you learn to pray?

? What sort of things do you pray for as a family? How do they correspond to the priorities Jesus gives His disciples?

? What are good times in the day to pray as a family?

? Think about each of your children. How are you helping each to pray? What do you pray with them daily?
What do you pray for them?

? When do you pray for something or someone outside of your home? How are your children involved in this?

? What would you like your kids to be praying for you?

a mission-centred family

11 A bigger family

Principle

We belong to two families.

 Consider this

Pete and Jan were part of a small church so they were involved in most things. And that meant their children, Sarah and Jack, were involved in most things as well. When Pete went early to set up each Sunday, Jack went with him. When Jan visited the housebound, Sarah went too. They had people in and out of their home a lot. Sometimes Sarah moaned about having yet another person round, but most of the time they enjoyed the adult company. With their own grandparents living some distance away, Harold and Anne had become kind of substitute grandparents – which seemed to suit both young and old. Plus Pete and Jan had benefited from their advice over the years.

There wasn't a youth group in the church. But John, a single guy in his twenties, took an interest in Jack, sometimes taking him fishing. Meanwhile Matt and "the other Sarah" had Sarah round most weeks for a movie and popcorn. They were the ones who had led her to Christ last year.

But Pete and Jan were worried. They'd just come back from a conference. Pete had been to a seminar on boundaries, where the speaker had stressed the need to protect family time. Jan had found other mums were surprised they hadn't moved to a church with a Christian youth group.

So they'd popped round for a chat with Harold and Anne. What did they think?

Biblical background
Read Mark 3 v 31-35

[?] Who are the family of Jesus?

[?] The words of Jesus were very shocking in His culture. How do they sound in your culture?

[?] What are the implications of this story for our priorities and allegiances?

Read all about it

Christians belong to two families. We're born into our biological families, but we're born again into God's family. We're children of our parents, but we're also children of God. And, as Jesus reminds us, our new divine family is our primary allegiance (Mark 3 v 31-35).

All societies have families. Of course, human families are not perfect; some are pretty dysfunctional. But God still intends children to be raised in families. We can't escape our families. We belong to them and they come with responsibilities.

But Christians are also adopted into a new family (Ephesians 1 v 5). It's our privilege to call God "Father" (Romans 8 v 15; Galatians 4 v 6). The church is described as God's household or family (1 Timothy 3 v 15). We're to treat one another and love one another in the church community as family members (Galatians 6 v 10; 1 Timothy 5 v 1-2). We belong to one another just as biological families belong to one another (Romans 12 v 5).

There'll be no marriage in the age to come. Instead we will all be God's children (Luke 20 v 34-36). The Bible story climaxes with the marriage of Christ to His bride, the church (Ephesians 5 v 25; Revelation 19 v 6-9; 21 v 2). Ultimately, there will be only one marriage and only one family.

So Christians belong to these two families at the same time.

Sometimes that creates tensions – especially with our extended biological family. They may have expectations of us that conflict with our commitment to our church family. After all, Jesus said: "I have come to turn "a man against his father, a daughter against her mother ... a man's enemies will be the members of his own household." Anyone who loves his father or mother more than me is not worthy of me" (Matthew 10 v 35-37).

We cannot hide behind our Christian commitment to escape responsibility for our own family (Mark 7 v 9-13; 1 Timothy 5 v 4,8). Nor can we let human family commitments stand in the way of following Christ (Mark 3 v 31-35; Luke 9 v 59-62).

But, while there are times when you need to make choices, it's important not to view your wider church family as a rival to your immediate biological family. Quite the opposite. To be a flourishing gospel-centred family, you need your church family. There's an old African saying which goes: "It takes a village to raise a child". Or we might say: "It takes a whole church to raise a child".

What might this involve?

1. **Include the people from the church family in your family time.** It's an indulgent myth that family time must be exclusive. Let people share in ordinary family meals, join in family celebrations, take part in trips out, play games with your children, cook for you and come along on family holidays. Be a family to single people.

2. **Involve your children in your hospitality.** Don't side-line them in favour of your guests. Get your children cooking and serving food. Include them in conversations. Encourage guests to interact with your children. Play games together – guests and children included. Think of hospitality not as a performance art, but including people in family life.

3. **Don't think of your family as self-contained or self-sufficient.**

You can't raise your children or nurture your marriage on your own. You need people to look after your children while you go on a date or a romantic weekend. You need people who can advise on feeding toddlers or handling teenagers. You need people who can tell you you're doing okay when it feels as if everything's unravelling.

4. **You need the wider church family for advice, encouragement and challenge.** Open your family life for other Christians to explore. From time to time, ask older Christians to give you honest feedback on what they see in your family life – especially if they've just spent time with you all.

5. **And you need to provide support to other families in your church family.** Being a single parent is especially tough. Not only is the parent-child ratio doubled, but there's next to no time off from children. We can't be a husband to a single mum or a father to her children. But we can be substitute uncles and aunts.

6. **"It is not good for the man to be alone," says God (Genesis 2 v 18).** His immediate solution in the Garden of Eden was marriage, but marriage is not an option for everyone or at every time. So, if you have the space, have someone live with you and be part of your family.

7. **Many people have not grown up with good models of family life.** They would really benefit from an opportunity to share in the life of a Christian family for a while before they start a family of their own.

8. **Think of ways you can involve your children in the life of your church – and not just in the children's or young people's ministry.** Can they accompany you when you do ministry? Can

they put out chairs or hand out song books? Can they visit the housebound?

9. **Encourage your children to build relationships with adult believers.** And build relationships with young people yourself. We've found relationships between young people, and Christians who are older than them but younger than their parents to be invaluable.

Questions for reflection

[?] What are the benefits of growing up with an extended Christian family?

[?] Where, if anywhere, do you feel the tension between your Christian family and your biological family?

[?] What are your obligations to your extended (biological) family? What responsibility should your children feel to their extended family? What responsibility do they feel?

[?] What has helped your children see beyond your immediate family?

[?] What stake do your biological and Christian families have in the way your kids are raised? How can they be partners with you in Christian parenting?

[?] Identify people in your church family that have a good relationship with your children, especially people older than your children. What could you do to encourage them or thank them?

[?] How do you open your home to the church family? Could you have someone live with you? Could you open your meal table more to people?

[?] Could you "adopt" a single person in your church?

[?] Think of your last three family celebrations, events or trips. Did you involve other people from the church family? Could you have done so? What about the next three family events?

[?] Alex: "I loved having people come and go in our home when I grew up – so many good times – talking , playing, laughing. Some are still friends with me today."
Harry: "I came to resent the many guests my parents had. I just wanted my parents to myself, but the guests always came first."
How can you ensure your children look back like Alex rather than Harry?

12 A serving family

Principle

Children are not the centre of the world.

Consider this

"Hey, Mary, we're holding a service in the local old people's home, the one near the supermarket. Would you be interested in helping out?"

"Er, maybe. What do you do?"

"Oh, nothing elaborate. Sing some hymns, pray, someone gives a short Bible message. Then we hand round cakes and chat with the residents."

"When is it?"

"Sunday afternoons."

"Ah, I'm afraid we usually take the children to the park then."

"Bring them along. The old folks love seeing children."

"I'm not sure. Besides, it's our family time. And, you know, family's important. Family first and all that."

"This is family time, no? Perhaps you could make some cakes for us. Get the children involved, perhaps."

"Maybe. But I don't think they'll be keen. I guess I could make some."

Pauline was listening in to the conversation. She paused. She wanted to say something, but what?

Biblical background
Read Mark 12 v 28-34

❓ What is your number one priority for your family?

❓ What does Jesus say is the most important commandment?

❓ How is the first commandment worked out in your family life and parenting?

❓ What about the second commandment?

❓ What evidence could your children bring to show that you believe these are the greatest commandments?

Read all about it

Our children are not the centre of the world. They're not the centre of our world. They're not even the centre of their world.

What is the number one priority for your family? Listen to the words of Jesus: "The most important [commandment] is this: "Hear, O Israel, the Lord our God, the Lord is one. Love the Lord your God with all your heart and with all your soul and with all your mind and with all your strength." The second is this: "Love your neighbour as yourself." There is no commandment greater than these" (Mark 12 v 29-31).

The centre of the world is God. Human beings were made for Him and to give Him glory. That means God is to be the centre of your family's world. And closely linked to that is a commitment to serving others. A gospel-centred family is a family that serves others to the glory of God.

Neighbours aren't just the people next door. When Jesus was asked: "Who is my neighbour?" he told the story of the good Samaritan (Luke 10 v 25-37). The teacher of the law who asked the question probably expected Jesus to say his obligations were to fellow Jews. But the story of the good Samaritan shows our neighbour is anyone we meet who needs our mercy. In a world with global links, we are neighbours with the people who produce our tea and sugar, whose sweatshop made our jeans or whose famine we hear about on the news. The Samaritan was good because he put mercy above racial and social boundaries.

The teacher of the law asked the question, Luke tells us, because he wanted to justify himself. He wanted to be able the tick the box. "Love for neighbour. Tick. Done." But we can't justify ourselves by ticking off a world of needy neighbours. The truth is we find justification in the gospel – in the finished work of Jesus. But those who have received divine mercy show that same love to others. Those who once served only themselves are freed to serve others in love. We can't finish the task of loving a world of needy neighbours, but we can start!

So being a gospel-centred family is about what you do "inside" your family, but it's a whole lot more than that. A family that's turned inwards is not a gospel-centred family. The gospel is good news. It's a message we share with others, beginning with our neighbours and extending to the ends of the earth (Acts 1 v 8).

When their good is not their good

So our children are not the centre of the world. Yet that's how we often treat them. We structure our lives around them. We may not give them everything they want. After all, we don't want to spoil them, we tell ourselves. But we do everything for them. Their good sets the agenda. We fit other things around them. We put their education above ministry opportunities. We live in nice neighbourhoods so they're not corrupted. Getting them to the church youth group matters more than other people's needs.

The irony is that doing everything for their good is not for their good! They learn that they come first, that their needs are paramount, that the world is there for them. In the west we are perhaps creating one of the most indulged generations ever.

If we put our children before serving God and others, then we make an idol of them. How will they learn to worship God as God if they see us worshipping them in place of God? We don't serve our children well by putting them at the centre of our lives, a space reserved for God alone.

Serving with your children

One of the best ways to teach your children to serve is to serve together as a family. Here are some ideas:

1. **Involve children in household chores.** Yes, it's true that most of the time it's easier and quicker to do it yourself. But getting the job done is not your priority. Teaching your children to serve is more important – if a lot slower!

2. **You need to model a servant attitude yourself.** Let your children see you putting other people's needs before your own. But remember, you serve your children by gently and graciously being in authority over them, to demonstrate God's loving authority. So be careful not to become their servant – otherwise they'll become indulged masters.

3. **Involve your children in evangelism.** When your church has evangelistic events, talk with your children about who you can invite. Talk with them about sharing the good news of Jesus with their friends. Model gospel enthusiasm: if your heart sinks at the thought of "evangelism", you'll quickly pass on this attitude to your children.

4. **Serve others with your children in the way you pray.** Don't just pray for family needs. Pray for neighbours, friends, your church, mission partners and world events.

5. **How can your family serve your local neighbours?** Is there someone in your street who would appreciate a visit or needs help with shopping, putting the rubbish out or their garden? Could one of your children do it or could you do it as a family?

6. **How can your family serve your distant neighbours?** Involve your children in buying fairly traded goods, recycling waste and linking with mercy ministries.

7. **When children say "But I want..." or "It's not fair...", don't try to persuade them going to the shops or washing up or having a guest is really going to be a lot of fun, really.** Simply remind them: "It's not your world and you're not God."

8. **Encourage your children to give money.** When our daughter asked about giving as a Christian, I punched a hole in the lid of a jam jar so she could put aside some of her pocket money. Another family regularly gave their children some money for them to give away to others.

9. **Serve other people in the way you talk about them.** We find Sunday lunch can be tricky because we're tempted to moan about people we've met. This teaches our children to be nice to someone's face, yet gossip about them behind their back.

10. **Praise the attitude of a servant heart whenever you can – in your children and in other people.** Let children see that this is a thing to be prized. The world around us looks down on service. But Jesus said that "whoever wants to become great among you must be your servant'. He Himself "did not come to be served, but to serve" (Mark 10 v 42-45; Philippians 2 v 1-11). Teach your children the meaning of true greatness.

Questions for reflection

? Audit your children's involvement in household chores. What do they do? What could they do? Do you need a rota or a list of responsibilities for each child?

? When do your children hear you prizing the greatness of service?

? Who are your neighbours? List the people you're linked with – locally and globally.

? Who are your needy neighbours? What could you do as a family to serve them?

? What opportunities do you have to share the good news of Jesus with your neighbours? What could you do as a family to reach them?

? What evangelistic events does your church have coming up? How could you involve your children in these events? How could you encourage your children to share the good news with their friends?

Ideas for action

Identify one regular act of service you could do with your children in your church or neighbourhood. Putting out chairs, tending someone's garden, visiting the housebound, for example.

There's a famous adage that no one says on their death-bed: "I wish I'd spent more time at the office." But it's also true that many will say on the Judgment Day: "I wish I hadn't indulged my children so much, teaching them that they were the centre of the world."

Further Reading

Tedd Tripp, **Shepherding a Child's Heart** (Shepherd Press, 1995)

Paul David Tripp, **Age of Opportunity: A Biblical Guide to Parenting Teens** (P&R, 2001)

Ann Benton, **Aren't They Lovely When They're Asleep?** (Christian Focus, 2003)

Timothy Sisemore, **Our Covenant with Kids: Biblical Nurture in Home and Church** (Christian Focus, 2008)

Tim Chester, **You Can Change: God's Transforming Power for Our Sinful Behaviour and Negative Emotions** (IVP, 2008)

John A. Younts, **Everyday Talk: Talking Freely and Naturally about God with Your Children** (Shepherd Press, 2004)

Alison Mitchell, **Table Talk** (The Good Book Company)

Brian Godawa, **Hollywood Worldviews: Watching Films with Wisdom and Discernment** (InterVarsity Press, 2002)

Denise George, **Teach your Children to Pray** (Christian Focus, 2004)

Daphne Spraggett with Jill Johnstone, **Window on the World, the children's version of Operation World** (Paternoster, 2001)

www.damaris.org.uk has an extensive collection of reviews, articles and discussion notes on movies, novels, music and television programmes from a Christian perspective.

Gospel-centred church
becoming the community God wants you to be

In *Gospel-centred church*, Steve Timmis and Tim Chester explain that gospel ministry is much more than simply evangelism. It is about shaping the whole of our church life and activities by the content and imperatives of the gospel. It is about ensuring that our church or group is motivated by and focused on the gospel, as opposed to our traditions. This workbook is designed to help clarify our thinking about how we should live our lives as the people of God.

Gospel-centred life
becoming the person God wants you to be

How can ordinary Christians live the truly extraordinary life that God calls us to? By focusing our attention on the grace of God shown to us in the gospel, everyday problems, familiar to Christians everywhere, can be transformed as the cross of Christ becomes the motive and measure of everything we do. *Gospel-centred life* shows how every Christian can follow the way of the cross as they embrace the liberating grace of God.

Gospel-centred marriage
becoming the couple God wants you to be

It's not just the famous "marriage passages" that shape a gospel-centred marriage, but the whole Bible-story of God's good creation, humanity's wicked rebellion and God's gracious redemption. This study guide focuses on how the Gospel shapes the practical realities of everyday life. Tim Chester lifts the lid on many of the common pressure points that modern couples face, and shows how a proper understanding of the Gospel can shape a response.

FOR MORE INFORMATION AND TO ORDER:
UK & Europe: www.thegoodbook.co.uk
N America: www.thegoodbook.com
Australia: www.thegoodbook.com.au
New Zealand: www.thegoodbook.co.nz

thegoodbook
COMPANY

At The Good Book Company, we are dedicated to helping Christians and local churches grow. We believe that God's growth process always starts with hearing clearly what He has said to us through His timeless word—the Bible.

Ever since we opened our doors in 1991, we have been striving to produce resources that honour God in the way the Bible is used. We have grown to become an international provider of user-friendly resources to the Christian community, with believers of all backgrounds and denominations using our Bible studies, books, evangelistic resources, DVD-based courses and training events.

We want to equip ordinary Christians to live for Christ day by day, and churches to grow in their knowledge of God, their love for one another, and the effectiveness of their outreach.

Call us for a discussion of your needs or visit one of our local websites for more information on the resources and services we provide.

UK & Europe: www.thegoodbook.co.uk
N America: www.thegoodbook.com
Australia: www.thegoodbook.com.au
New Zealand: www.thegoodbook.co.nz

UK & Europe: 0333 123 0880
N America: 866 244 2165
Australia: (02) 6100 4211
New Zealand (+64) 3 343 1990